Contents

wild animals

Wild animals

zwijsen
bdyslexie
font
is the typeface used in this book

WAYLAND

Camilla Lloyd

First published in paperback in 2016 by Wayland
Copyright © Wayland 2016

Wayland
An imprint of
Hachette Children's Group
Part of Hodder & Stoughton
Carmelite House
50 Victoria Embankment
London EC4Y 0DZ

Editor: Elizabeth Brent
Designer: Amy McSimpson

Dewey number: 428.1-dc23

ISBN   978 1 5263 0348 6
Library eBook ISBN   978 0 7502 8535 3

Printed in China

10 9 8 7 6 5 4 3 2 1

Picture acknowledgements: All images, including the cover image, courtesy of Shutterstock.com, except: p4-5 © Johan Swanepoel/iStockPhoto, p10-11 © Roberto A Sanchez/iStockPhoto; p19 © Getty Images/Giles Breton

The website addresses (URLs) included in this book were valid at the time of going to press. However, it is possible that contents or addresses may change following the publication of this book. No responsibility for any such changes can be accepted by either the author or the Publisher.

Wayland is a division of Hachette Children's Books,
an Hachette UK company.
www.hachette.co.uk

These are
wild animals.

There are lots of different
kinds of wild animals.

monkey

This is a monkey.

Monkeys like to swing from trees.

elephant

These are elephants.

Elephants have long noses called trunks.

rhinoceros

This is a rhinoceros.

Rhinoceroses have a horn on their nose.

parrot

These are **parrots**.

Parrots have brightly coloured feathers

tiger

This is a **tiger**.

A baby **tiger** is called a cub.

12

zebra

These are **zebras.**

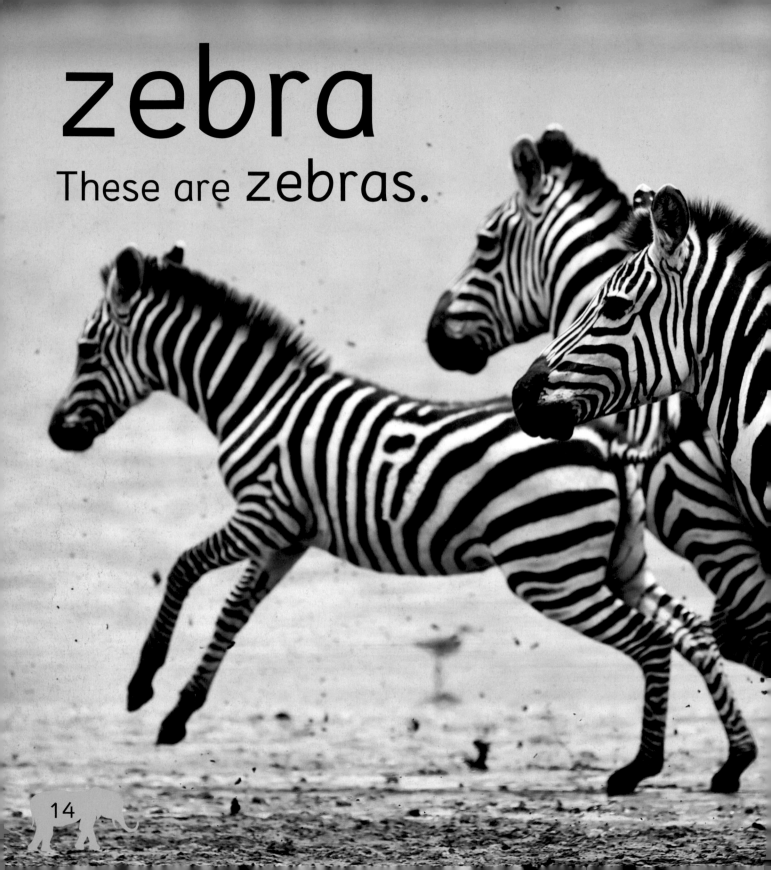

Zebras have striped coats.

15

snake

This is a snake.

A **snake's** body is smooth and covered with scales.

crocodile

This is a crocodile.

Crocodiles have very sharp teeth.

17

lion

This is a lion.

Lions have a very loud roar.

giraffe

This is a giraffe.

Giraffes have very long necks.

Picture quiz

Which animals have these things?

striped coats

long necks

bright feathers

long trunks

What pages are they on?

Index quiz

The index is on page 24.
Use the index to answer these questions.

1. Which page shows a **tiger**?
   What are baby tigers called?

2. Which page shows a **monkey**?
   What do monkeys like to do?

3. Which page shows a **rhinoceros**?
   What do rhinoceroses have
   on their noses?

4. Which page shows a **snake**?
   What kind of skin does a snake have?

23

Index

Answers

Picture quiz: Giraffes are on pages 20 & 21. Zebras are on pages 14 & 15. Parrots are on pages 10 & 11. Elephants are on page 8.
Index quiz: 1. Page 13, cubs; 2. Page 7, swing from trees; 3. Page 9, a horn; 4. Page 16, smooth and scaly.